Essential Questionnaires For The 13 Eligibility Categories

NAVIGATING IDEA

A Kelly Neal, Esq.

Library of Congress Control Number: 2025905193

ISBN: 979-8-9929441-2-9
Cover design by A. Kelly Neal, Esq.
Printed in the United States of America
For more information, visit www.SSAdisability.org

Disclaimer

This book is dedicated to every educator who has ignored a child's struggle, denied services to make their job easier, or hidden behind red tape instead of doing what's right. You know exactly who you are. Your negligence has stolen opportunities, broken spirits, and forced parents into brutal, uphill battles just to secure what their children were legally—and morally—owed.

To the parents who have been gas lit, dismissed, and told to 'trust the process' while watching their child suffer—this book is your ammunition. Use it to tear down the excuses, expose the failures, and force a system built on indifference to do its damn job. Because if they won't fight for your child, you will. And you will win."

Power To Our Pupils

To everyone who contributed to this book, thank you.
Your contributions do not go unnoticed or unappreciated.

For far too long, parents have been forced to navigate a broken system—one that claims to serve children with disabilities but instead buries them in bureaucracy, delays, and denial. I have seen firsthand how schools manipulate the process, how educators—whether out of ignorance or apathy—deny children the support they desperately need, and how parents are left feeling helpless, exhausted, and alone in their fight for justice.

I wrote this book because enough is enough.

This is not just a guide; it is a tool for empowerment. It is designed to arm parents, advocates, and educators who actually care with the knowledge they need to cut through the confusion and demand what is rightfully owed to every child under the law. The IDEA eligibility process should not be a battle of wills, nor should parents have to become legal experts just to ensure their child receives an education that meets their needs. Yet, here we are.

My hope is that this book will serve as both a shield and a sword: a shield for parents who need protection from the system's endless roadblocks, and a sword to cut through the excuses, the misinformation, and the outright failures that keep children from getting the education they deserve.

If you are a parent reading this, know that you are not alone. You are not crazy. You are not asking for too much. Your child has rights, and those rights are non-negotiable.

And to those in the system who refuse to do their jobs—consider this your warning. Parents are learning. Parents are fighting. And parents will win.

—**A. Kelly Neal, Esq.**

You and pediatricians play a crucial role in ensuring that children receive the services, supports, and accommodations necessary for them to succeed in their educational environments. These questionnaires are specifically designed to align with the Individuals with Disabilities Education Act (IDEA), providing a structured approach to assessing and supporting children in obtaining eligibility for an Individualized Education Program (IEP).

I encourage you to integrate these questionnaires into your work to help children access the educational resources and opportunities they rightfully deserve.

Thank you for your commitment to advocating for and improving the lives of these children.

A Kelly Neal, Esq.

TABLE OF CONTENTS

The **Individuals with Disabilities Education Act (IDEA)** is a landmark federal law that ensures children with disabilities receive a free appropriate public education (FAPE) in the least restrictive environment (LRE). It was first enacted in 1975 and has been reauthorized several times, with the most recent amendment in 2004.

IDEA outlines a framework for identifying, evaluating, and providing services to children with disabilities. The law is designed to level the playing field for students who have physical, emotional, cognitive, or developmental disabilities, ensuring they have equal access to education alongside their peers.

Key Elements of IDEA:

1. **Free Appropriate Public Education (FAPE)**
   Schools must provide an education tailored to the individual needs of each child with a disability at no cost to the parents. This includes the provision of necessary services, supports, and accommodations.

2. **Least Restrictive Environment (LRE)**
   Students with disabilities should be educated with their non-disabled peers to the greatest extent possible. They should only be removed from general education settings if their disability is so severe that it prevents them from making progress in that setting.

3. **Individualized Education Program (IEP)**
   IDEA mandates that every eligible child with a disability has an IEP, which is a customized education plan that outlines the specific supports and services the child needs to succeed. The IEP must be developed and reviewed annually by a team, including the child's parents, teachers, and specialists.

4. **Procedural Safeguards**
   Parents have a right to participate in decision-making processes regarding their child's education, and they are provided with safeguards to ensure their child's rights are protected. These include the right to challenge decisions, access records, and request due process hearings if necessary.

5. **Evaluation and Eligibility Determination**
   IDEA outlines specific procedures for evaluating children suspected of having disabilities. Evaluations must be conducted in a timely, non-discriminatory, and thorough manner. Children are deemed eligible for special education services if they meet one of the 13 eligibility categories defined by IDEA.

6. **Parent and Teacher Collaboration**
   A fundamental principle of IDEA is the active involvement of parents in their child's education. Schools are required to collaborate with parents and provide regular updates on the child's progress. Parents have the right to be part of the IEP team and to challenge decisions if they disagree with the proposed educational plan.

7. **Transition Planning**
   As children with disabilities approach adulthood, IDEA requires schools to create transition plans starting at age 16 (or younger, depending on the state). These plans focus on helping students transition from school to post-school life, including higher education, vocational training, and employment.

Purpose and Impact:

IDEA's framework is designed to ensure that children with disabilities receive the education they deserve, tailored to their specific needs. The law promotes equity in education by providing safeguards for students and families, requiring school districts to meet the educational needs of students with disabilities, and holding schools accountable for their progress.

IDEA's goal is not just to provide an education, but to enable children with disabilities to develop the skills and confidence necessary to thrive in society, ultimately fostering independence and success in adult life.

The process of determining eligibility for an Individualized Education Program (IEP) under the Individuals with Disabilities Education Act (IDEA) involves several steps to ensure that a child with a disability receives the appropriate services and supports needed to succeed academically. Here's an overview of how eligibility is determined:

1. Referral for Evaluation

The process typically begins when a child is referred for an evaluation to determine if they have a disability and if they require special education services. This referral can be made by a parent, teacher, or other professional who believes the child may have a disability. The referral should be based on observed difficulties in the child's academic performance or behavior, or other signs that suggest the child may need additional support.

Key Points:

- Parents can request an evaluation at any time.
- The school must respond to the referral and obtain parental consent before proceeding with the evaluation.

2. Evaluation Process

Once the referral is made, the child will undergo a comprehensive evaluation to assess if they meet the criteria for one of the 13 disability categories outlined in IDEA. The evaluation is conducted by a team of professionals, which may include special education teachers, school psychologists, speech therapists, and other specialists.

The evaluation must be:

- Non-discriminatory: Conducted in a way that doesn't favor one group over another, such as using culturally and linguistically appropriate tests.
- Timely: The evaluation process must be completed within 60 days (or a timeframe specified by the state).
- Comprehensive: It must assess all areas of suspected disability, including academic, cognitive, emotional, and physical needs.
- Parental Consent: Parents must give written consent for the evaluation before it can proceed.

3. Eligibility Determination

After the evaluation, the team of professionals, including the child's parents, will review the results to determine if the child has a disability that falls within one of the 13 categories specified by IDEA. These categories include, but are not limited to, autism, learning disabilities, emotional disturbance, speech/language impairments, and intellectual disabilities.

The eligibility criteria are:

- The child must have one or more of the disabilities listed in IDEA. These include both physical and mental impairments that significantly affect the child's ability to perform in school.

- The disability must affect the child's ability to succeed in a general education setting without additional supports. This could mean difficulty with academic achievement, social interactions, communication, or behavior.

- **The child must require special education services** in order to make progress in school. This is assessed based on the child's ability to access the general education curriculum with or without accommodations and modifications.

If the child is found eligible, the team will proceed to develop an Individualized Education Program (IEP) that outlines the child's specific educational needs, goals, and the services required to support their learning.

4. Parental Involvement and Consent

Throughout the eligibility determination process, parents must be involved in discussions and decisions. They have the right to:

- Participate in the evaluation and IEP meetings.
- Be informed of the evaluation results.
- Consent to or refuse the proposed evaluations and services.
- Request an independent educational evaluation (IEE) if they disagree with the school's assessment.

5. Development of the IEP

If the child is determined eligible for special education services, the team will create an IEP. The IEP is a written plan that includes:

- Present levels of performance: A description of how the child is doing in their academic and functional skills.

- Measurable goals: Clear, specific goals that the child will work toward during the year.

- Services and supports: Details about the special education services, accommodations, modifications, and related services the child will receive.

- Placement: The least restrictive environment (LRE) where the child will be educated (i.e., in a regular education classroom with supports or in a more specialized setting).
- Progress monitoring: How the child's progress will be measured and reported to the parents. The IEP must be reviewed and updated annually or more frequently if necessary to ensure the child's needs are being met.

6. Reevaluation

IDEA requires that all students who have an IEP be reevaluated at least once every three years (or more often if requested). The reevaluation helps to assess the child's progress and determine whether they still meet eligibility criteria for special education services.

Summary

IEP eligibility is determined through a process that involves a referral, comprehensive evaluation, and a collaborative team decision-making process. The key factor in determining eligibility is whether the child's disability significantly impacts their ability to succeed in school without specialized support. Once eligible, an IEP is created to outline the services and accommodations necessary to help the child succeed. Parents play an essential role throughout the process, ensuring that their child's needs are met and advocating for their rights.

ROLE OF EVALUATIONS AND ASSESSMENTS IN IEP ELIGIBILITY

Evaluations and assessments are at the heart of determining whether a child is eligible for special education services under the Individuals with Disabilities Education Act (IDEA). These processes help to identify the specific needs, strengths, and challenges of a child with a disability and provide the information necessary for creating an effective Individualized Education Program (IEP). Below is an overview of their critical role:

1. Identifying Disabilities

Evaluations and assessments are used to determine if a child has one of the disabilities listed under IDEA's 13 eligibility categories (such as autism, learning disabilities, speech impairments, emotional disturbance, etc.). A thorough evaluation helps professionals and parents understand whether the child's difficulties in school are due to a disability and which category of disability the child may fall under.

2. Establishing the Child's Educational Needs

Once a disability is identified, assessments are used to pinpoint the child's specific academic, behavioral, social, and functional needs. These evaluations help to:

- Identify areas where the child may need additional support, such as reading, writing, math, behavior, social skills, etc.
- Assess the child's ability to access the general education curriculum.
- Determine whether modifications, accommodations, or related services (like speech therapy or occupational therapy) are necessary for the child to succeed.

3. Determining the Impact on Academic Performance

The central goal of the evaluation is to assess how the child's disability impacts their ability to succeed in a general education environment. This includes:

- Understanding the severity of the disability and how it affects the child's academic performance and social interactions.
- Evaluating how the child responds to different instructional strategies and supports.
- Identifying whether the child requires specialized services to benefit from education and whether their needs can be met within the general education setting or require a more specialized educational setting.

4. Providing Baseline Data for IEP Development

Evaluations and assessments provide the baseline data needed to develop a child's IEP. This data includes:

- The child's current levels of academic achievement and functional performance.
- Specific strengths and weaknesses in areas such as reading, math, social skills, emotional regulation, and more.

- Clear measures of the child's progress in comparison to their peers, which is critical for setting measurable IEP goals.

5. Guiding Decision-Making for Services and Supports

Once the child's educational needs are assessed, the evaluation helps determine the specific services and supports that should be included in the IEP. These may include:

- Related services: Speech therapy, occupational therapy, counseling, physical therapy, etc.
- Accommodations and modifications: Adjustments in classroom settings, teaching strategies, or testing methods (e.g., extended time, quiet spaces).
- Behavioral interventions: Plans to address behavior concerns or social-emotional challenges.
- Instructional approaches: Strategies or materials tailored to the child's learning style.

6. Ensuring Non-Discriminatory Assessment

Under IDEA, evaluations must be non-discriminatory, which means they should:

- Be fair and culturally appropriate, taking into account the child's linguistic background and cultural differences.
- Use multiple methods and sources of data, including observations, academic records, teacher reports, and parental input, to avoid bias.
- Provide accurate results by using assessments that are valid, reliable, and appropriate for the child's age and disability type.

7. Parental Involvement and Consent

Parents are key partners in the evaluation process. They must give written consent before any evaluation is conducted, and they have the right to:

- Be involved in discussions about which evaluations and assessments are needed.
- Receive a full explanation of the results and how they will be used to determine eligibility and inform the IEP.
- Request an independent educational evaluation (IEE) at public expense if they disagree with the school's evaluation.

8. Reevaluation

IDEA requires that students who are eligible for special education services be reevaluated at least every three years (or more frequently if necessary). The reevaluation helps to:

- Assess whether the child's needs have changed.
- Determine whether the child still meets the eligibility criteria for special education services.
- Make adjustments to the child's IEP based on their progress or emerging needs.

9. Types of Evaluations and Assessments

The evaluation process typically involves multiple types of assessments, including but not limited to:

- Standardized tests: To assess cognitive abilities and academic skills.

- Observations: To evaluate the child's behavior, interactions, and functioning in different environments (classroom, playground, home).

- Parent and teacher input: Surveys, questionnaires, and observations to provide insight into the child's abilities and needs.

- Psychological assessments: To measure cognitive abilities, mental health, and emotional functioning.

- Speech and language assessments: To evaluate communication skills, articulation, and comprehension.

- Behavioral assessments: To evaluate specific behaviors that may require intervention.

Conclusion

Evaluations and assessments are the foundation of determining IEP eligibility and creating a tailored educational plan. These tools help ensure that children with disabilities receive the appropriate services and supports to meet their unique needs. They guide educational professionals and parents in making informed decisions about the best way to support a child's learning, ensuring that every child receives a fair chance at success in the educational system

Procedural safeguards are a critical component of the Individuals with Disabilities Education Act (IDEA), designed to ensure that the rights of children with disabilities and their parents are protected throughout the special education process. These safeguards provide parents with important rights and mechanisms for holding schools accountable when it comes to providing a free appropriate public education (FAPE) for their child.

Here's an overview of the key procedural safeguards under IDEA:

1. Parent Participation

Parents have the right to be active participants in decisions about their child's education. This includes the right to:

- Participate in meetings regarding their child's evaluation, IEP development, placement decisions, and progress.

- Request a meeting to discuss any concerns about their child's education or to review and amend the IEP.

- Be informed in advance about meetings and provided with sufficient time to prepare.

- Access educational records: Parents have the right to inspect and review all educational records related to their child's evaluation and placement.

2. Prior Written Notice

Schools must provide parents with prior written notice when they propose or refuse to:

- Evaluate or reevaluate their child.

- Change their child's eligibility for special education services.

- Make changes to the child's IEP or placement.

This notice must include a detailed explanation of:

- The action the school is proposing or refusing.

- The reasons for that action.

- Any evaluations, assessments, or reports that were used to make the decision.

3. Informed Consent

Before conducting an evaluation or making significant changes to a child's educational plan, the school must obtain informed consent from the parents. This means that parents must understand and agree to the proposed evaluation or service. The school cannot proceed without this consent unless certain conditions are met.

4. Independent Educational Evaluation (IEE)

If parents disagree with the school's evaluation, they have the right to request an Independent Educational Evaluation (IEE) at public expense. The IEE allows parents to obtain an evaluation by an independent expert of their choice.

- If the school disagrees with the parent's request for an IEE, the school can request a due process hearing to justify its evaluation.
- If the IEE is deemed appropriate, the results must be considered by the IEP team.

5. Dispute Resolution Processes

IDEA provides parents with several ways to resolve disagreements with the school regarding their child's education:

- Mediation: A voluntary process in which an impartial third party helps the parents and school resolve disputes. Mediation is free of charge.
- Due Process Hearings: If mediation doesn't resolve the dispute, parents can request a due process hearing, which is a formal legal proceeding. A hearing officer listens to both sides and makes a binding decision.
- State Complaint Process: Parents can file a formal complaint with the state education agency if they believe their rights under IDEA have been violated.
- Civil Action: As a last resort, parents can file a civil lawsuit in state or federal court to resolve disputes over FAPE or other violations of IDEA.

6. Stay-Put Provision

The stay-put provision ensures that a child's current educational placement remains unchanged during the resolution of a dispute. This means that if a disagreement arises about changes to a child's IEP or placement (e.g., school suspension, placement in a different classroom), the child must remain in their current educational setting until the dispute is resolved—unless the parents and school agree otherwise. **7. Access to Educational Records**

Parents have the right to access all records related to their child's education, including:

- Evaluation and assessment records.
- Progress reports and records of meetings related to the child's education.
- Correspondence related to the child's education, such as emails, letters, or notes from meetings. Schools are required to provide access to these records in a timely manner and may not withhold them except for specific exceptions, such as when certain information is confidential.

8. Confidentiality of Information

IDEA requires schools to protect the privacy and confidentiality of students' personal and educational information. This includes:

- Limiting access to personal records to those with a legitimate need to know.

- Ensuring that any personal or identifiable information is protected from unauthorized disclosure.

- Giving parents the right to request corrections to records if they believe there is inaccurate or misleading information.

9. Right to a Free Appropriate Public Education (FAPE)

Parents have the right to ensure that their child receives a Free Appropriate Public Education (FAPE), which includes:

- The right to challenge decisions that deny their child an appropriate education.

- The right to ensure that their child's IEP is followed and that the child receives the services they need to succeed.

10. Resolution Session

Before proceeding to a due process hearing, parents and the school district are required to meet in a resolution session. This meeting allows both parties to discuss the issue and attempt to resolve the dispute without a formal hearing. It must occur within 15 days of the due process complaint being filed.

Summary

Procedural safeguards under IDEA are essential for protecting the rights of children with disabilities and their parents. They ensure that parents have a voice in their child's education, that decisions are made transparently, and that disputes are resolved fairly. These safeguards empower parents to advocate for their child's educational needs, whether by requesting an evaluation, participating in IEP meetings, or pursuing dispute resolution options if necessary. The goal is to guarantee that children with disabilities receive the appropriate education they are entitled to under the law.

CLIENT NAME:_____ Date of Exam:_____

VISUAL IMPAIRMENT INCLUDING BLINDNESS
34 CFR 300.8(c)(13)

Does your patient have an impairment in vision?   Yes_____ No_____

Is your patient's vision corrected?   Yes_____ No_____

Despite corrective measures does your patient's vision adversely affect

educational performance?   Yes_____ No_____

Does your patient have partial sight [ ] or partial blindness [ ]?   Yes_____ No_____

Physician Signature_____Name:_____

CLIENT NAME: _____ Date of Exam: _____

TRAUMATIC BRAIN INJURY
34 CFR 300.8(c)(12)

Does your patient have an acquired injury to the brain caused by an external

physical force?   Yes_____ No_____

Has this injury resulted in total [ ] or partial [ ] functional disability?   Yes_____ No_____

Yes_____ No_____
Has this injury resulted in total [ ] or partial [ ] psychosocial impairment?

Has this injury resulted in total [ ] or partial [ ] functional disability and
psychosocial impairment?   Yes_____ No_____

Has the functional disability [ ], psychosocial impairment [ ] or both [ ] adversely
affected your patient's educational performance?   Yes_____ No_____

Is the traumatic brain injury the result of an open head injury?   Yes_____ No_____

Is the traumatic brain injury the result of a closed head injury?   Yes_____ No_____

Does the traumatic brain injury result in impairment in cognition?   Yes_____ No_____

Does the traumatic brain injury result in impairment in language?   Yes_____ No_____

Does the traumatic brain injury result in impairment in memory?   Yes_____ No_____

Does the traumatic brain injury result in impairment in attention?   Yes_____ No_____

Does the traumatic brain injury result in impairment in reasoning?   Yes_____ No_____

Does the traumatic brain injury result in impairment in abstract thinking?   Yes_____ No_____

Does the traumatic brain injury result in impairment in judgment?   Yes_____ No_____

Does the traumatic brain injury result in impairment in problem-solving?   Yes_____ No_____

Does the traumatic brain injury result in impairment in sensory ability?   Yes_____ No_____

Does the traumatic brain injury result in impairment in perceptual ability?   Yes_____ No_____

Does the traumatic brain injury result in impairment in motor ability?   Yes_____ No_____

Does the traumatic brain injury result in impairment in psychosocial behavior?   Yes_____ No_____

Does the traumatic brain injury result in impairment in physical functions?   Yes_____ No_____

Does the traumatic brain injury result in impairment in information processing? Yes_____ No_____

Does the traumatic brain injury result in impairment in speech?   Yes_____ No_____

Is the brain injury congenital?   Yes_____ No_____

Is the brain injury degenerative?   Yes_____ No_____

Was the brain injury induced by birth trauma?   Yes_____ No_____

Physician Signature_____Name:_____

CLIENT NAME: _____Date of Exam:_____

SPEECH OR LANGUAGE IMPAIRMENT
34 CFR 300.8(c)(11)

Does your patient have a speech impairment?   Yes_____ No_____

Does your patient have a language impairment?   Yes_____ No_____

Does your patient's communication disorder include stuttering?   Yes_____ No_____

Does your patient's communication disorder include impaired articulation?   Yes_____ No_____

Does your patient's communication disorder include voice impairment?   Yes_____ No_____

Is your patient's educational performance adversely affected as a result of
these impairments?   Yes_____...No_____

Physician
Signature_____Name:_____

CLIENT NAME: _____Date of Exam: _____

SPECIFIC LEARNING DISABILITY
34 CFR 300.8(c)(10)

Does your patient have a disorder in one or more of the basic psychological processes involved in understanding or in using language?   Yes_____ No_____

Does this disorder affect written language?   Yes_____ No_____

Does this disorder affect spoken language?   Yes_____ No_____

Does it manifest itself in an imperfect ability to:

Listen?   Yes_____ No_____

Think?   Yes_____ No_____

Speak?   Yes_____ No_____

Read?   Yes_____ No_____

Write?   Yes_____ No_____

Spell?   Yes_____ No_____

Do mathematical calculations?   Yes_____ No_____

Does your patient have perceptual disabilities?   Yes_____ No_____

Does your patient have a brain injury?   Yes_____ No_____

Does your patient have minimal brain dysfunction?   Yes_____ No_____

Does your patient have dyslexia?   Yes_____ No_____

Does your patient have developmental aphasia?   Yes_____ No_____

Are your patient's learning problems the primarily the result of:

Visual issues?   Yes_____ No_____

Hearing issues?   Yes_____ No_____

Motor disabilities?   Yes_____ No_____

Intellectual disability?   Yes_____ No_____

Emotional disturbance?   Yes_____ No_____

Environmental issues?   Yes_____ No_____

Cultural issues?   Yes_____ No_____

Economic disadvantage?   Yes_____ No_____

Physician

Signature_____Name:_____

CLIENT NAME: _____Date of Exam: _____

OTHER HEALTH IMPAIRMENT
34 CFR 300.8(c)(9)

Does your patient have a limited strength?	Yes_____	No_____
Does your patient have a limited vitality?	Yes_____	No_____
Does your patient have limited alertness?	Yes_____	No_____
Does your patient have heightened alertness to environmental stimuli?	Yes_____	No_____
Does this heightened alertness result in limited alertness in with respect to the educational environment?	Yes_____	No_____
Is the limited alertness due to chronic or acute health problems?	Yes_____	No_____
Does the health problem include asthma?	Yes_____	No_____
Does the health problem include attention deficit disorder?	Yes_____	No_____
Does the health problem include attention deficit hyperactivity disorder?	Yes_____	No_____
Does the health problem include diabetes?	Yes_____	No_____
Does the health problem include epilepsy?	Yes_____	No_____
Does the health problem include a heart condition?	Yes_____	No_____
Does the health problem include hemophilia?	Yes_____	No_____
Does the health problem include lead poisoning?	Yes_____	No_____
Does the health problem include leukemia?	Yes_____	No_____
Does the health problem include nephritis?	Yes_____	No_____
Does the health problem include rheumatic fever?	Yes_____	No_____
Does the health problem include sickle cell anemia?	Yes_____	No_____
Does the health problem include Tourette syndrome?	Yes_____	No_____
Do the health problems adversely affect educational performance?	Yes_____	No_____

Physician Signature_____Name:_____

CLIENT NAME: _____Date of Exam:_____

ORTHOPEDIC IMPAIRMENT
34 CFR 300.8(c)(8)

Does your patient have a severe orthopedic impairment?   Yes_____ No_____

Does the severe orthopedic impairment adversely affect a child's
educational performance? (ex. limit ability to participate in PE)   Yes_____ No_____

Is the impairment caused by a congenital anomaly or disease?
(e.g. poliomyelitis, bone tuberculosis)?   Yes_____ No_____

Does the impairment(s) have other causes (e.g., cerebral palsy,
amputation, and fractures or burns that cause contractures)?   Yes_____ No_____

Physician

Signature_____Name:_____

CLIENT NAME: _____Date of Exam: _____

MULTIPLE DISABILITIES
34 CFR 300.8(c)(7)

Does your patient have concomitant impairments (such as intellectual
Disability/blindness or intellectual disability/orthopedic impairment)?   Yes_____ No_____

Are your patient's multiple disabilities deaf-blindness?   Yes_____ No_____

Does the combination cause such severe educational need that
your patient cannot be accommodated in special education
programs solely for one of the impairments?   Yes_____ No_____

Physician Signature_____Name:_____

CLIENT NAME: _____Date of Exam: _____

INTELLECTUAL DISABILITY
34 CFR 300.8(c)(6)

Does your patient have significant sub-average general intellectual functioning? Yes_____ No_____

Does your patient also have deficits in adaptive behavior?   Yes_____ No_____

Did these deficits manifest during the developmental period?   Yes_____ No_____

Do these deficits adversely affect your patient's educational performance?   Yes_____ No_____

Physician Signature_____Name:_____

CLIENT NAME: _____Date of Exam: _____

HEARING IMPAIRMENT
34 CFR 300.8(c)(5)

Does your patient have an impairment in hearing?   Yes_____ No_____

Is this impairment in hearing permanent?   Yes_____ No_____

Is this impairment in hearing fluctuating?   Yes_____ No_____

Does this impairment adversely affect your patient's educational performance?   Yes_____ No_____

Physician Signature_____Name:_____

CLIENT NAME: _____ Date of Exam: _____

EMOTIONAL DISTURBANCE
34 CFR 300.8(c)(4)(i)

Has your patient had emotional disturbance over a long period of time?   Yes_____ No_____

Does your patient have emotional disturbance to a marked degree?   Yes_____ No_____

Does your patient's emotional disturbance adversely affect their
educational performance?   Yes_____ No_____

Does your patient have an inability to learn that cannot be explained by
intellectual, sensory, or health factors?   Yes_____ No_____

Does your patient have an inability to build or maintain satisfactory
interpersonal relationships with peers and teachers?   Yes_____ No_____

Does your patient have inappropriate types of behaviors or feelings
under normal circumstances?   Yes_____ No_____

Does your patient have general pervasive mood of unhappiness or depression? Yes_____ No_____

Does your patient have a tendency to develop physical symptoms or
fears associated with personal or school problems?   Yes_____ No_____

Does your patient have schizophrenia?   Yes_____ No_____

Is your patient socially maladjusted?   Yes_____...No_____

Physician Signature_____ Name:_____

CLIENT NAME: _____Date of Exam: _____

DEAFNESS
34 CFR 300.8(c)(3)

Does your patient have a hearing impairment?   Yes_____ No_____

Is the hearing impairment so severe that your patient is impaired in
processing linguistic information through hearing?   Yes_____ No_____

Regardless of amplification, does this impairment in processing linguistic
information through hearing adversely affect your patient's
educational performance?   Yes_____ No_____

Physician Signature_____Name:_____

CLIENT NAME: _____ Date of Exam: _____

DEAF-BLINDNESS
34 CFR 300.8(c)(2)

Does your patient have a concomitant hearing and visual impairments?   Yes_____ No_____

Does the combination cause severe communication needs?   Yes_____ No_____

Does the combination cause severe developmental needs?   Yes_____ No_____

Yes_____ No_____

Does the combination cause educational needs?

Is you patient unable to be accommodated in special education programs
solely for children with deafness or children with blindness?   Yes_____ No_____

Physician Signature_____Name:_____

CLIENT NAME: _____ Date of Exam: _____

AUTISM
34 CFR 300.8(c)(1)(i)

Does your patient have a developmental disability?   Yes_____ No_____

Does this developmental disability affect verbal communication?   Yes_____ No_____

Does this developmental disability affect nonverbal communication?   Yes_____ No_____

Does this developmental disability affect social interaction?   Yes_____ No_____

Was this developmental disability generally evident before age three?   Yes_____ No_____

Does this developmental disability affect your patient's educational performance?   Yes_____ No_____

Does your patient engage in repetitive activities?   Yes_____ No_____

Does your patient engage in stereotypical movements?   Yes_____ No_____

Are these repetitive activities or stereotypical movements
resistant to environmental change?   Yes_____ No_____

Are these repetitive activities or stereotypical movements
resistant to change in daily routines?   Yes_____ No_____

Are these repetitive activities or stereotypical movements
resistant to unusual responses to sensory experiences?   Yes_____ No_____

Is the patient's educational performance adversely affected
primarily because the child has an emotional disturbance?   Yes_____ No_____

Has you patient manifested characteristics of autism after age three?   Yes_____ No_____

Physician Signature_____Name:_____

Requesting special education services for a child under the Individuals with Disabilities Education Act (IDEA) is an important step in ensuring that children with disabilities receive the support they need to succeed in school. Parents, guardians, or anyone involved in the child's education can initiate the process. Here's a step-by-step guide on how to request special education services:

1. Observe and Document Concerns

Before making a formal request, it's important to observe and document the child's difficulties in school. This could include issues related to academic performance, behavior, communication, social interactions, or physical challenges. Keep records of:

- Specific areas where the child is struggling.

- Any patterns or changes over time.

- Teacher or school reports, including grades, test results, and behavior observations.

- Notes from meetings with the school or teachers.

This documentation will help provide a clear picture of the child's needs when making the request.

2. Contact the School

The first step in requesting special education services is to contact the school. You should reach out to the following people:

- Your child's teacher or special education teacher (if applicable) to discuss your concerns and ask for their input.

- The school principal or the special education coordinator to request a formal evaluation.

- School counselor or psychologist, if there are behavioral or emotional concerns.

Clearly communicate your concerns about your child's difficulties in school and express your interest in evaluating whether your child might be eligible for special education services under IDEA.

3. Submit a Written Request for an Evaluation

Under IDEA, parents can request an evaluation to determine if their child is eligible for special education services. While a verbal request can begin the process, it is recommended that you submit a written request for an evaluation to ensure that it is documented properly.

A written request should:

- Include your child's name, age, grade, and school.

- Outline your concerns and why you believe your child may need special education services.

- Request & consent to an evaluation to assess whether your child qualifies for services under IDEA.

You can address this written request to the school's special education coordinator, principal, or school psychologist.

Sample Request Letter:

[Date]

[School's Name]

Attention: [Special Education Coordinator/Principal]

Dear [Name or Title],

I am writing to request a formal evaluation of my child, [Child's Full Name], who is currently in [Grade] at [School Name]. I have concerns about [briefly describe concerns, e.g., academic performance, behavior, social interaction, etc.], and I believe an evaluation is necessary to determine whether my child may need special education services under IDEA. This letter serves at my consent for evaluation.

I would appreciate your prompt attention to this request and look forward to discussing the next steps.

Sincerely,

[Your Name]

[Your Contact Information]

4. Consent for Evaluation

Once you've submitted your written request, the school must provide you with a consent form to evaluate your child. Under IDEA, the school cannot proceed with the evaluation without written consent from the parent or guardian. The consent form will explain:

- The types of evaluations the school plans to conduct.
- What areas will be assessed (e.g., academic skills, emotional health, cognitive abilities, etc.).
- The purpose of the evaluation.

After you sign and return the consent form, the school will arrange for the evaluation to take place. This process must be completed within a certain time frame (usually within 60 days of receiving consent).

5. Evaluation and Eligibility Determination

The school will conduct a comprehensive evaluation to determine if your child qualifies for special education services. The evaluation will assess your child's strengths, needs, and any disabilities they may have. It may include:

- Standardized tests and assessments.
- Observations of your child in different settings.
- Interviews with teachers, parents, and other professionals.
- Academic records and work samples.

After the evaluation is completed, the school must hold an eligibility meeting with you (and other relevant professionals) to review the results and decide whether your child is eligible for special education services under one of IDEA's 13 disability categories.

6. Requesting an IEP Meeting

If your child is found eligible for special education services, the school will work with you to create an Individualized Education Program (IEP). This is a legal document that outlines your child's specific needs, goals, and the services that will be provided to help them succeed in school.

You have the right to be an active participant in the IEP development process. At the IEP meeting, you will:

- Discuss your child's strengths and challenges.
- Set measurable goals for your child's academic and functional progress.
- Determine the services (e.g., speech therapy, occupational therapy) and accommodations (e.g., extra time for tests) that your child will receive.
- Decide on the best educational placement for your child (e.g., inclusion in a regular classroom or specialized setting).

7. Monitor and Review the IEP

After the IEP is developed, the school will implement the services and supports outlined in the plan. The IEP must be reviewed at least annually to assess progress and make any necessary adjustments. You have the right to:

- Request an IEP review meeting at any time if you believe the plan isn't working for your child.
- Monitor your child's progress and request updates from the school on how your child is doing.

8. Dispute Resolution

If you disagree with the evaluation results, the proposed IEP, or any aspect of the services being offered, IDEA provides several ways to resolve disputes, including:

- Mediation: A neutral third-party helps facilitate a discussion between you and the school.
- Due Process Hearing: A legal proceeding where an impartial hearing officer listens to both sides and makes a binding decision.
- State Complaint Process: A formal process to file complaints about violations of IDEA.

Summary

Requesting special education services begins with a formal request for an evaluation. Once the school receives consent, a comprehensive evaluation will be conducted to determine if your child qualifies for services under IDEA. If your child is found eligible, an IEP will be developed, outlining the services and supports they need. Parents are essential partners throughout the process and have the right to monitor, review, and dispute decisions if necessary to ensure their child receives the services they need to succeed.

The Individualized Education Program (IEP) process is a critical component of special education under the Individuals with Disabilities Education Act (IDEA). It ensures that children with disabilities receive a tailored education that meets their unique needs. The IEP process is a multi-step procedure that involves parents, educators, and other professionals working together to create and implement a personalized educational plan for the child. Below is an overview of each step in the IEP process.

1. Requesting an Evaluation

The IEP process begins when a parent, teacher, or other professional requests an evaluation to determine whether a child has a disability and qualifies for special education services. This request can be made in writing to the school, which is required to respond within a specific timeframe (usually 60 days).

- If the child is found to have a disability that impacts their education, the next step is to develop an IEP.
- If the evaluation results indicate that the child is not eligible for services, the parent has the right to appeal or request further evaluations.

2. Evaluation and Eligibility Determination

Once the evaluation is requested and parental consent is obtained, the school conducts a comprehensive evaluation of the child's educational needs. This evaluation typically includes:

- Psychological assessments (e.g., cognitive and academic testing).
- Behavioral assessments.
- Speech, language, and occupational therapy evaluations (if applicable).
- Teacher reports and classroom observations.

After the evaluation, a team (including parents) will meet to determine whether the child qualifies for special education services under one of the 13 disability categories outlined by IDEA. If the child qualifies, the team moves on to the development of the IEP.

3. Developing the IEP

Once a child is found eligible for services, the IEP team (which includes parents, teachers, special education staff, and relevant specialists) comes together to develop the IEP. The IEP is a legally binding document that outlines the services and supports the child will receive.

Key components of an IEP include:

- Present Levels of Performance (PLP): A description of the child's current academic and functional performance, including strengths and areas of need.
- Measurable Annual Goals: Specific, measurable goals for the child to achieve within a year. These goals focus on academic skills, functional skills, and other areas of development.
- Services and Supports: A detailed outline of the special education services and related services (e.g., speech therapy, counseling, etc.) the child will receive. This also includes the type, frequency, and duration of these services.
- Accommodations and Modifications: The accommodations and modifications the child will need to access the general education curriculum (e.g., extra time on tests, seating arrangements).
- Placement: A determination of the child's educational placement (e.g., mainstream classroom, special education classroom, or a more restrictive setting).
- Measurement of Progress: How the child's progress will be measured and how parents will be informed about the child's progress towards the annual goals.

The IEP must be developed within 30 days of determining eligibility for services, and parents must be actively involved in all decisions made during this process.

4. Parental Consent

After the IEP is developed, the school must obtain written consent from the parents before implementing the plan. This ensures that parents are in agreement with the proposed services and placement. If parents do not consent, the school cannot proceed with the IEP.

5. Implementation of the IEP

Once the IEP is approved, the school will begin to implement the services and supports outlined in the plan. The child will receive the specific interventions, accommodations, and modifications designed to help them succeed in the least restrictive environment (LRE).

- The general education teacher, special education teacher, and any other staff involved are responsible for following the IEP and providing the services outlined.
- Parents will receive regular updates (e.g., quarterly reports or progress reports) on the child's progress toward the goals set in the IEP.

6. Monitoring and Review of Progress

The IEP team is responsible for monitoring the child's progress toward their goals. The IEP should be reviewed regularly, and parents should be informed of the child's progress at least once a year.

- The team should determine whether the child is making adequate progress toward their goals. If the child is not progressing as expected, the IEP may need to be revised.
- The IEP must be updated at least once every 12 months to reflect changes in the child's needs or progress.

7. Annual IEP Review

At least once a year, the IEP team will hold an annual review meeting to discuss the child's progress, assess the effectiveness of the current IEP, and make any necessary changes to goals or services. This is an opportunity to adjust the IEP to better meet the child's needs based on the data gathered from the previous year. Parents are encouraged to participate in these meetings and provide input into how their child is performing and whether the current goals are still appropriate.

8. Reevaluation

IDEA requires that children receiving special education services undergo a reevaluation at least once every three years, or more frequently if the child's needs change or if requested by the parents. The purpose of the reevaluation is to assess:

- Whether the child continues to meet the eligibility criteria for special education.
- Whether the child's educational needs have changed, requiring new services, goals, or supports.
- Whether any adjustments need to be made to the child's IEP based on updated information.

Reevaluations include gathering new data on the child's performance and may involve updated assessments and input from parents, teachers, and specialists.

Summary

The IEP process is designed to ensure that children with disabilities receive personalized and effective educational support. It begins with an evaluation to determine eligibility and continues through the development of an IEP tailored to the child's needs. The IEP is implemented, monitored, and reviewed regularly, and adjustments are made to ensure the child's success. Parents play an integral role throughout the process, from requesting services to providing feedback during meetings and monitoring progress. The goal of the IEP process is to provide a free appropriate public education (FAPE) that prepares children with disabilities for success in school and beyond.

Advocating for a child with disabilities can be a challenging and emotional process, but it is essential in ensuring that the child receives the support and services they need under the Individuals with Disabilities Education Act (IDEA). As a parent, you are your child's strongest advocate. Here are some tips to help you effectively advocate for your child's education and ensure they get the services they deserve:

1. Understand Your Rights and Responsibilities

Knowledge is power. Take the time to learn about the Individuals with Disabilities Education Act (IDEA) and your rights as a parent. Understanding the law, your child's rights to special education services, and the special education process will empower you to advocate more effectively.

- Know your child's rights to a Free Appropriate Public Education (FAPE).
- Familiarize yourself with the 13 disability categories under IDEA.
- Learn how to request evaluations and what your child's Individualized Education Program (IEP) should include.

2. Document Everything

Keep thorough records of all communications and interactions with the school. This includes emails, letters, meeting notes, and phone conversations. Detailed documentation can be invaluable in resolving disputes or tracking your child's progress over time.

- Write down dates and times of important conversations.
- Keep copies of your child's school reports, evaluations, and assessments. ☐
  Maintain a log of meetings and the outcomes of those meetings.

3. Be Involved and Stay Engaged

You are your child's best advocate, so staying actively involved in their education is crucial. Attend all IEP meetings, and actively participate in decisions about your child's services and placement.

- Ask questions if you don't understand something.
- Review and monitor your child's IEP regularly to ensure that it is being followed.
- Request regular updates on your child's progress toward their IEP goals, either through progress reports or direct communication with teachers.

4. Build a Support Network

Advocacy can be more effective when you are supported by others who understand the process. Connect with other parents, advocacy groups, or professionals who can offer guidance and support.

- Join local or online support groups for parents of children with disabilities.
- Collaborate with other parents to share experiences and strategies.
- Reach out to advocacy organizations that provide resources, training, and even legal support (e.g., Parent Training and Information Centers (PTIs)).

5. Communicate Effectively

Clear, respectful communication is key when advocating for your child. Always approach school staff with the goal of finding a solution, rather than creating conflict.

- Be respectful and professional in all interactions.
- Clearly state your concerns and offer specific examples of how the school can address them.
- Listen carefully to the school staff's perspective and try to collaborate on solutions.
- Use written communication whenever possible to ensure clarity and documentation.

6. Know the Power of the IEP Team

The IEP team is made up of individuals who are responsible for planning your child's education. You, as the parent, are a vital member of this team, and your input is essential in creating a plan that will best meet your child's needs.

- Be prepared to actively contribute to IEP meetings by providing information about your child's strengths, challenges, and needs.
- Don't be afraid to ask for changes to the IEP if you feel it isn't working or isn't aligned with your child's needs.
- Understand that the IEP team must work together to create a plan that is in your child's best interest, so you have the right to disagree and request changes.

7. Be Assertive but Calm

Advocacy often requires persistence. If the school is not providing the services your child needs, don't be afraid to ask for more or escalate the issue. However, it's important to remain calm and focused on finding solutions, rather than getting frustrated or emotional.

- Ask for meetings if you are not satisfied with your child's progress or placement.
- Be prepared to advocate at higher levels (e.g., requesting a meeting with the school principal, district representatives, or seeking mediation or a due process hearing if necessary).
- Know when to escalate: If necessary, don't hesitate to reach out to your state's Department of Education, a special education advocate, or a special education attorney.

8. Know When to Seek Help

Sometimes, the IEP process or the school may be unresponsive to your concerns. In these cases, it may be helpful to seek outside assistance.

- Special Education Advocates: These are professionals who specialize in helping parents navigate the IEP process and can represent you in meetings or hearings.
- Attorneys: If you believe your child's rights are being violated and you cannot resolve issues through the school, a special education attorney can help you understand the legal options available.
- Mediation and Due Process: If a disagreement arises that cannot be resolved, mediation or filing for a due process hearing can help resolve conflicts.

9. Prepare for Meetings

When attending IEP meetings or meetings with school staff, preparation is key. Be clear on what you want to achieve and be ready to present your concerns and needs for your child.

- Create an agenda or list of points you want to discuss.
- Bring your child's documentation (test results, previous IEPs, progress reports).
- Set clear goals for the meeting and know your desired outcomes.
- Stay focused on your child's needs: While you may encounter differing opinions, always keep the conversation focused on what is best for your child's education.

10. Trust Your Instincts

As a parent, you know your child better than anyone else. Trust your instincts about what they need and what works for them. If something doesn't seem right or if you feel your child is not receiving adequate support, speak up. Don't let others dismiss your concerns—your voice matters.

Summary

Advocating for your child's special education needs involves being well-informed, proactive, and persistent. By understanding your rights, documenting your child's progress, staying engaged with the IEP process, and working collaboratively with the school, you can ensure that your child receives the appropriate services and support they need to succeed. Be prepared to assert your child's rights, build a support network, and seek outside help when necessary. Most importantly, stay focused on your child's best interests, and never be afraid to speak up for what they need